JOYVILLE
GLEELAND
Cheerbury
Mt. OPTIMISM
DELIGHTBURG
Glad Point
DELIGHTBURG
Glad Point
JOYVILLE
Bliss Springs
Bliss Springs
Cheerbury
JOYVILLE
Glad Point
Mt. OPTIMISM
HAPPY TOWN
GLEELAND
GLEELAND
Cheerbury
HAPPY TOWN
Mt. OPTIMISM
DELIGHTBURG
GLEELAND
JOYVILLE

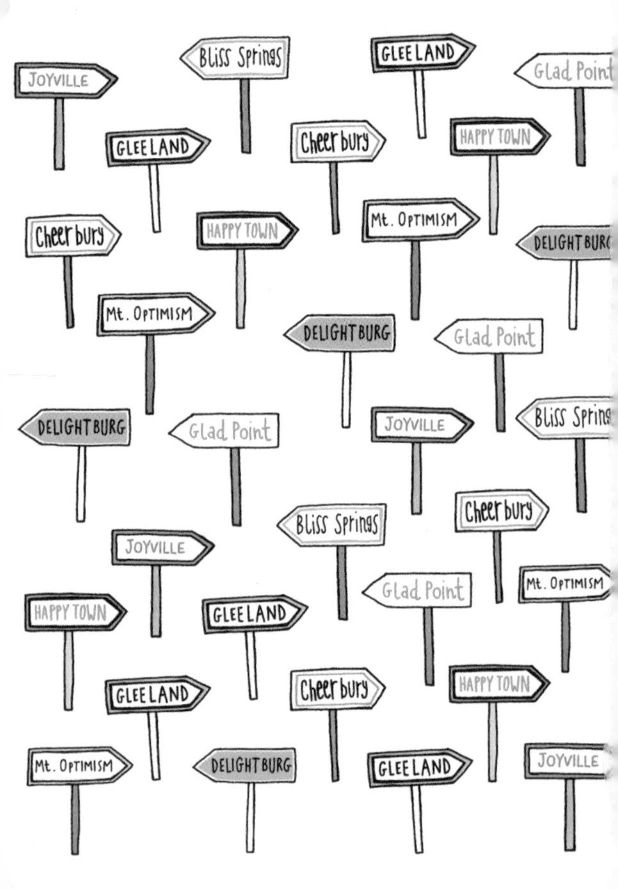
JOYVILLE
Bliss Springs
GLEELAND
GLEELAND
Cheerbury
HAPPY TOWN
Cheerbury
HAPPY TOWN
Mt. OPTIMISM
Mt. OPTIMISM
DELIGHTBURG
Glad Point
DELIGHTBURG
Glad Point
JOYVILLE
Bliss Springs
Cheerbury
JOYVILLE
Glad Point
Mt. OPTIMISM
HAPPY TOWN
GLEELAND
GLEELAND
Cheerbury
HAPPY TOWN
Mt. OPTIMISM
DELIGHTBURG
GLEELAND
JOYVILLE

JOYVILLE

Created and published by Knock Knock
1635-B Electric Avenue
Venice, CA 90291
knockknockstuff.com

Illustrations by Gemma Correll

ISBN: 978-160106681-7
UPC: 825703-50046-2

10 9 8 7 6 5 4 3 2 1

100 Reasons to Panic about Being Single

KNOCK KNOCK®
VENICE, CALIFORNIA

The good ones are already taken.*

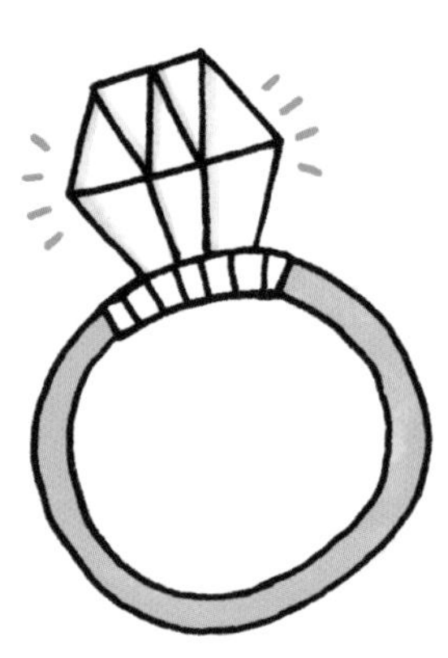

*If that's true, why are you single?

You'll live alone.*

*And never have to ask anyone
to turn the game on (or off).

Everyone will always ask you if you're seeing someone.*

*You are seeing someone: yourself.

You'll have to sleep alone.*

*Your bed will be free of snoring.

If you can't find someone, maybe you're too picky.*

*You're not picky, you're discriminating.

If you can't find someone, maybe you're too selfish.*

*You're not selfish, you're just not desperate.

You'll get set in your ways.*

*You'll experience the joys of never compromising.

First dates are terrifying.*

*They're also ripe with possibility.

Your shopping cart is kind of a bummer.*

*Cat food, soup, chocolate, wine: sounds like all the major food groups are taken care of.

You've heard "It's not you, it's me" a few too many times.*

*It's not you—it's them.

11.

Another income sure would be nice.*

*Yeah, but no one will wonder where all the money goes.

You'll watch too much TV.*

*You won't have to share space on the DVR with anyone.

You'll give up and stop taking care of yourself.*

*Ice cream for breakfast—delicious!

You're too shy—you'll never meet anyone.*

*You're mysterious and alluring.

You'll hook up with random people out of desperation.*

*You'll avoid that awkward "Are we exclusive?" talk.

You meet people—they just happen to be married.*

*You've got good taste—unfortunately, so do their spouses.

You'll have to attend weddings by yourself.*

*No worries about making sure your date has something appropriate to wear.

Everyone will try to set you up.*

*You'll be an expert at the where-are-you-from, what-do-you-do, do-you-have-any-hobbies part of getting to know people.

You'll become obsessed with taking selfies for your online dating profile.*

*It's all the fun of a modeling career—none of the stress.

14:52
MY PHOTOS
Share

You'll get a ton of cats.*

*Snuggling, companionship, and someone to talk to: it's a win-win.

The older you get, the smaller the pond gets.*

*But there's a whole younger world out there waiting for you.

You're all dressed up with no place to go.*

*Surely a night in deserves a fancy dress.

You're tired of being the break-upper.*

*Better to dump than to get dumped.

You're tired of being the break-uppee.*

*Better to get dumped than to deal with the guilt of dumping.

"Party of one" is so depressing.*

*Not having to make small talk is awesome.

Your friends will start having kids and you'll feel left out.*

*You'll get to be the freewheeling aunt or uncle.

You're always the bridesmaid, never the bride.*

*But never the miserable married person!

You're always the groomsman, never the groom.*

*But never the miserable married person!

Your biological clock is ticking.*

*Hit the snooze button.

You won't have a date for New Year's Eve. Or Valentine's Day. Or...*

*You'll save yourself the overpriced prix fixe meal surrounded by a bunch of suckers.

You'll never have sex.*

*Abstinence is the safest sex, after all!

Sharing a home with someone would be nice.*

*You won't have to give up those fantastic flea market finds.

You'll take a bunch of different classes and still not meet someone.*

*But you now can kayak, grow a terrarium, and cook a mean pasta Bolognese.

You'll resort to speed dating.*

*Better to make a quick decision than suffer through a painful date.

Your aunt will continually ask when you're going to settle down.*

*Your answer? "When I decide not to settle."

No one will send you flowers.*

*You can send yourself flowers—and sign the card, "Love, your secret admirer."

You'll vacation alone.*

*No one will complain about an itinerary full of museums instead of the beach (or vice versa).

PARIS
ooh la la!

You'll be the only single person at holiday dinners.*

*You'll get to sit at the kids' table. It's more fun.

Cooking for one is sort of a bummer.*

*The leftovers can be your lunch—for a week.

If you never marry, you'll miss out on wedding gifts.*

*You'll also miss out on the non-registry gifts that you feel guilted into keeping, even though they're ugly and not-very-useful.

No one will take care of you when you're sick.*

*No one has to hear you cough, sneeze, and wheeze either.

When your friends aren't around, who will you talk to?*

*You'll have a reason to strike up conversations with strangers.

You'll be the token single friend.*

*You'll remind your coupled friends what freedom looks like.

Interpreting texts from potential partners will get tiresome.*

*You're learning another language.

You can't ever take advantage of bulk pricing at warehouse clubs.*

*Really, who can eat twenty pounds of oatmeal?

You could really use some help around the house.*

*Watch enough YouTube tutorials and you'll figure out how to do everything yourself.

You'll lack romance in your life.*

*Relationships are full of unromantic things. Like bills.

Your married friends will only talk about married couple stuff.*

*They'll get a vicarious thrill from your stories about dating.

Your parent friends will only talk about parent stuff.*

*They'll get a vicarious thrill from your stories about sleep.

You'll read cheesy self-help books, hoping to "fix yourself."*

*Who said there's something wrong with you?

You'll have to make major decisions all by yourself.*

*Isn't that sort of empowering?

In the dark of night, you'll look up partners from the past "just to see what they're up to."*

*You're honing your detective skills.

Your family will bug you about living alone.*

*They'll always find something to bug you about.

You'll need to psych yourself up before going on blind dates.*

*You'll be like Rocky—but hopefully less sweaty.

You'll be a single mom.*

*Why are you worrying? Single moms are hot.

You'll be a single dad.*

*Why are you worrying? Single dads are hot.

You're dying to plan a wedding.*

*You're sparing yourself that killer stress.

Valentine's Day will suck.*

*You won't have to pretend to like those wilted roses or cheap chocolate.

If you hurt yourself and no one's around, they'll find you dead in your house years later.*

*Maybe you'll inspire one of those unsolved mystery shows!

Who will deal with bugs and critters?*

*Get a carnivorous plant—it's a plant and a pet in one!

Who will make sure you don't leave the house with two different socks?*

*Wearing mismatched socks shows you've got an unconventional sense of style.

No one will be around to scratch your back or rub your feet.*

*And no one will complain about doing those things for longer than 30 seconds.

You won't get any extra-special gifts on your birthday.*

*You can give yourself the gift of whatever you want—no hints required.

You'll have to attend weddings by yourself.*

*It'll allow you to hook up with out-of-town guests.

Your home will turn into a bachelor pad.*

*Those black leather couches look so wrong—but feel so right.

Your home will turn into a bachelorette pad.*

*If you spill on your white sofa, the only person you'll have to blame is yourself.

You'll have to make your own morning coffee.*

*Or you'll be a regular at a coffee shop—eventually they might even greet you by name.

You won't have someone to stay up all night with.*

*More like fall asleep while watching old sitcoms.

You won't be able to tell anyone your secrets, fears, or desires.*

*You won't need to find a hiding place for your diary.

No one's around to tell you how hot you are.*

*You can always walk by a construction site.

You won't have anything to contribute when a conversation with friends turns to relationships.*

*They'll be jealous of the lack of conflict in your life.

You'll get weird.*

*You won't have to hide your quirks.

There's no one to share the driving with on road trips.*

*You get to pick the snacks, the stops, and the music.

You'll wake up alone.*

*You won't have to be nice to anyone before you have coffee.

Your fear of commitment will cripple you.*

*You've committed to fear—that takes tenacity.

You'll want to play the field—forever.*

*Variety is, after all, the spice of life.

You'll start talking to yourself.*

*Who's more interesting than you?

You'll only meet jerks and losers.*

*You'll get skilled at ending dates quickly.

You'll be invisible.*

*You can stop trying so hard.

You'll have to admit you don't have a "plus-one."*

*You're saving the party planner money!

You'll never find your soul mate.*

*Research has shown everyone has more than one soul mate.

You won't feel like you're part of a team.*

*You can join a kickball league—you might even get matching shirts!

Who will zip up your dress?*

*It's a good time to meet the neighbors, including that hottie down the block.

You won't get invited to any dinner parties because hosts only want couples.*

*Hosts just want interesting, charming people. You are interesting and charming, aren't you?

You'll regret the one who got away.*

*Oh, please. Keeping to the fish metaphor, there are plenty of 'em in the sea.

People will note that you don't wear a wedding ring—and judge you.*

*They're probably just admiring your manicure.

People will note that you don't wear a wedding ring—and try to pick you up.*

*And what's wrong with that?

No one will notice if you don't get home safely.*

*And no one will notice if you are out all night!

You'll always get hit on in bars.*

*You'll have someone else buying your drinks. Score!

You'll get called a spinster.*

*You can turn the stereotype on its head.

You'll get called a cranky old man.*

*You probably should stop yelling at kids to get off your lawn, anyway.

You'll have no one to play board games with.*

*You'll be awesome at solitaire.

Your local delivery place recognizes your voice on the phone.*

*See, someone needs you.

You'll get first-date fatigue.*

*You'll be like an FBI profiler, instantly sensing if it'll work out or not.

Your attached friends will always ask you, "How are you still single?"*

*You can put them in their place with "How do you have a boyfriend?"

You'll get stood up.*

*Awesome. You can go home and take those Spanx off.

You used to wonder who you might meet at the grocery store or the dog park—now you just don't care.*

*Hey, sweatpants are comfortable.

It's nice to cuddle before you fall asleep.*

*Why cuddle when you can hog all the pillows and sleep diagonally?

You might not ever find "The One."*

*Plenty of people claim they did—and divorced.